Travails of Trevale

T. Loretta "Spirit" Tucker

Earth, Fire & Wind

Publisher's Note- This book was not edited by CLF Publishing, LLC. The editing was done by an outside entity to the author's satisfaction.

Published by CLF Publishing, LLC. 3281 Guasti Road, Seventh Floor, Ontario, CA 91761. (760) 669-8149.

ISBN# 978-0-9884237-5-6

Printed in the United States of America.

DEDICATIONS

To: Those who are or are curious about the proud, eager, anxious, tempted, passive, determined, partial, tired, frustrated, intimidated, heavy laden children of God, who at times seem to un-attach themselves from the direction of the promised rewarding days, days of Quite Storms; those accepting life's expected and unexpected, yet travailing on for the sake of: "It is written…" The Salvation of Travails:

Ecclesiastes 3:10

I have seen the travail, which God hath given to the sons of men to be exercised in it.

Lamentations 3:5

He hath builded against me, and compassed me with gall and travail.

Jeremiah 4:31

For I have heard a voice as of a woman in travail, and the anguish as of her that bringeth forth her first child, the voice of the daughter of Zion, that bewaileth herself, that spreadeth her hands, saying, Woe is me now! for my soul is wearied because of murderers.

Micah 4:10

Be in pain, and labour to bring forth, O daughter of Zion, like a woman in travail: for now shalt thou go forth out of the city, and thou shalt dwell in the field, and thou shalt go even to Babylon; there shalt thou be delivered; there the LORD shall redeem thee from the hand of thine enemies.

Galatians 4:19

My little children, of whom I travail in birth again until Christ be formed in you.

Be unto you for the birth of New Life.

ACKNOWLEDGEMENTS

First to God for life, wisdom and power; I can do all things through Christ, which strengthens me (Philippians 4:13). To my mom, for her steadfast guidance and directions. To my dad, my sister and my brothers, for being just who they are while applying their supportive abilities. To my grandparents for prayers, example setting and support, Family and Friends for listening continuously to my enter thoughts which I spoke aloud often, My ex-husbands for experiencing life with me and assisting in bringing forth five wonderful children. To my children for empowerment and inspiration. to my shepherd's for spiritual teaching and counseling. to my spiritual families for association and prayers.

Author's Memo   Biography vs. Autobiography

Many already have asked and criticized about my title which presents my book as being a biography and not an auto-biography. As an opening page, I have chosen to input the Webster definition and encyclopedia findings of biography which relates deeply to the deliverance of these books: *Travails of Trevale* and all its volumes.

A biography is a detailed description or account of someone's life. It entails more than basic facts (education, work, relationships, and death), a biography also portrays a subject's experience of these events. Like a profile or curriculum vitae (résumé), a biography presents a subject's life story, highlighting various aspects of his or her life, including intimate details of experience, and may include an analysis of a subject's personality.

Biographical works are usually non-fiction, but fiction can also be used to portray a person's life. One in-depth form of biographical coverage is called legacy writing. Biographical works in diverse media—from literature to film—form the genre known as a biography.

An authorized biography (or official biography) is written with the permission, cooperation, and, at times, participation of a subject or a subject's heirs. An autobiography is about a life of a subject, written by that subject or sometimes with a collaborator. (Webster's Dictionary - Wikipedia, the free encyclopedia)

There is to come soon, the written story of "Trevale": a life story autobiography of the author.

Section Contents

I

Early Life

This is how it all started; born Black American Native of Compton, California part of the United States of America, back in 1970s I was fortunate to be perfectly made body mind and soul to the most beautiful intelligent and motivating Mom and the most original (OG) dad. You see right about now most people begin to judge. Compton! Near Watts, neighboring the LBC (Long Beach City) oh my God (OMG)!

All my life I wondered about segregation within our nation. With the separation within communities, I imagined it was something like tribal settings. I kind of grew to accept concepts and views of what was set by society: diverse, poor, unstable, dysfunctional, sick, violent, cruel and uneducated areas of great misfortune. Politicians were called in to address issues and concerned regarding environment and crime. African Americans begin to migrate to the city of Compton during the second great migration.

Myself am not only from the African American descendent culture, but I am descended also with white and Indian traits just two generations down, so I was not burns into the slave man conceptions and mentality which many imposes on the darker skinned individuals. Yet I was born into a new generation of slavery which in my mind still captivates violence as well as develops and nurture a lack of self well.

Both my parents were hard workers and self-sufficient, even before my birth. Birthing me in their early twenties, I must say full of energy they brought forth a unique healthy baby girl. Turning four, I could remember moving into our own first two bedroom two car garage house. This house was blessed to have beautiful landscape settings.

The floral settings were so divine and with a father who worked as a gardener and land scraper it stayed fresh looking nicely trimmed all the time. We had a lemon tree, orange tree, grapefruit tree, and a grape vine which was in two sections of the front and back yard. Then behind a brick fenced wall was another large section of yard which produced one apple tree, two apricots trees and a bee hive.

Yes a "bee hive", one of my biggest tortures during my life as I grew from 8-12 years in this house was hanging cloths on the cloths line which set right off from the orange tree which was next to the grape vine, ruler yards away from the bee hive which was embedded on the side of the old tool shack. My dad removed it and even specialists were called out, but that dang bee hive kept coming back.

As a child being blessed to stop any ice cream or doughnut truck which passed by, I didn't know I appeared to the bees as a sweet smelling treat. Each time my mom would call for me to hang the cloths, it would be over one hour fighting to shoo away the bees, which never worked, and yes the bees won every time sending me running leaving my basket of cloths behind.

Oh well I was a kid, so I did what kids do went back to playing, leaving the laundry undone. So what happens after that, punishment time! See I don't know about most homes, but in my home my mother believed in spare the rod and you spoil the child, in addition to; Proverbs 10:13, "in the lips of him that hath understanding wisdom is found; but a rod is for the back of him that is void of understanding." So I guess understanding was to be whipped into you. Hmmmm? Now don't get me wrong regarding my statements, we are going somewhere with this. Remember these are the Travails of Trevale where victory always prevails.

Another verse Proverbs13:24, delivers it like this, "he that spareth his rod hateth his son; but he that loveth him chasteneth him..." So I guess in an act of demonstrating love and punishing me for not finishing the laundry I had to bare the rod. As if the bees weren't enough. It didn't teach me then, but I now know how all those actions play together, do they make since now that I am older, "no" but

I took victims of societal development where as we live by what was given and taught to use.

My grandparents disciplined with the rod and so did my parents. Even I disciplined my children with the rod (a belt) until those exaggerated allegations developed. It was then when I begin to seek a more profound understanding of the word. What I was able to do after studying Moses and the rod and Ezekiel and the scroll was to paraphrase, bringing forth the revelation that the rod of Moses symbolized trust and faith in God whom sent him, just as Ezekiel Could not necessarily eat and digest the scroll, but the instructions signified allowing the message to marinate inside of the body so that the message would become a part of his nature. So outside of accepting scriptural jesters which symbolized the rod as a item to inflict pain hurt or bruises amongst our children, I symbolized the rod to be the word of God, the Holy Bible which deliveries the commandments in which believers are to live.

The use of a physical rod as a method of discipline really set the curse of violence in my home throughout life. I wish rode (word) disciplining could have been taught to my parents and their parents before them. I could be not 100% right, but I do believe violence begins at home. We have husbands beating wives, wives beating husbands all in the name on love. Then we have parents whipping children. And so on and so on. This at times is said to be all in the name of love and correction.

II

Joined with Siblings

I am blessed to have one sister and two brothers. Lucky me, I am the oldest. My mother bore three, my father bore of four. Unlike many families from back in the day's diverse areas of Compton, there wasn't much rivalry between my siblings and I. Now don't get me wrong we had our run of the meals, but nothing which escalated to involve pastors, priest, police, weapons, nor indication of sibling abuse.

See I didn't mention it before but I feel I'm blessed, I feel I was born blessed to a blessed family with even more blessings to come. Another thing that may need to be mentioned is my position as "Daughter of a King", this position has placed me in the acceptance of "Queen of a King on top of a Hill". Even being black and raised out of Compton I always felt unique, gifted, talented and successful. I thought I'd mention that because soon enough there will be a flip in that concrete notion. But as a big sister I felt on top of the world.

Ok back to the real world. My parents; mother especially operated successfully at giving us our independence from one another as she helped us grow together leaning and trusting in each other. Unlike Cain and Abel in Genesis 4:9 when the lord asked Cain where is your brother Abel? And Cain reply was," I don't know; am

I my brother's keeper? We were taught to symbolize that we were the keepers of our siblings and that is what I teach my children today. "Yes you are your brother's keeper." Now being disobedient toward that I feel one may require a rode type discipline, but for not finishing laundry, Naaaa! I think we could have talked that over. Anyhow under the guardianship, love, kindness and caring support of my mother; since of course my father went off on a new venture 'bachelorship', my siblings and I formed a unity of oneness whereas we done the best we could to look out for one another and watch each other's front and back.

III

Division

Oh boy here we go embarrassing some tragedies of real life. I have found examples of and believe that the major heart breaks within families, groups, and in communities is birthed through division. Though my parents done what they could to sustain an undividable life style our family's tower still broke. My parents divorced when I was twelve years old. They were good at covering up the end cause I never seen it coming. Thru there were parent fighting's; verbal, physical and otherwise, I never truly believed the end would come.

This end brought about tremendous negative effects on me, even till this day. Being the oldest and a teenager, undergoing parent separations and divorce brings about unimaginable circumstances and burdens. These circumstances and burdens begin causing me to act out in the worst of a rebellious nature; lying, stealing, fighting and even sex, yes sex before being found of my soul mate.

Excuse the shame as I bow my head but yes those were some of the treacherous sins I plagued. In addition to demonstrating the negative affects that my parents' abusive relationship and their unexpected divorce had on me at home. I even demonstrated the affects over to family member's homes and even at the baby sitters. I also took many of these negative behaviors to school. I still

23

remember the last day as if it was today that ended my parent's marriage.

My dad has Hands in the Kitchen, meaning he could really cook and favor food, and on that last day I could recall my dad preparing my sister and I one of his stove cooked juicy burgers with the chunky chopped green peppers & onions, seasoned to the taste and some fries. The worst of my imagination occurred when what had transpired the night before brought a change to life as I had grown to know and accept it as.

The Big Separation then Divorce (1982). My parents must have both been fed up, and apparently neither could fake it no more, my mom came home and declared "That was it"! My dad packed and moved on. I knew one day it may happen, but still never believed it would. Though I love my mother as a daughter should; and my best interest has always been in her hands, I was a daddy's girl. The separation tore me apart and even today thirty years later I am still broken, set free, but still broken. For at times those diverse situations have fallen upon me as well.

For years it was not easy for my mother, coping with paying and maintaining the bills along with the responsibility of raising three children. There was much stress and depressions within our home like many endure today, but we knew how to cover it up. This tends to be a natural reaction within our society; covering things up, that is. Later I'll explain how God uses that to an advantage for His/our sake. Casting all our care on him.... 1 Peter 5:7 states "casting all your cares upon him for he careth for you". For the anxious, the New International Version reads "cast all your anxiety on him because he cares for you". And for the worried, the New Living Translation states "give all your worries and cares to God for he cares about you". But till one comes into the knowledge of how this works, it's just plain old stress, depression, anxiety and worry, which still when un-dealt with or not dealt with properly causes, high/low blood, chronic pain, fatigue and doubt. Not to mention the many other effects and illnesses related to these stressor elements. So with all these broken factors and misfortune we were taught and demonstrated to pressed on.

IV

Travail

The English word travail originated from a French word meaning heavy labor. Eventually, travail also came to be used to refer to childbirth, hence the roundabout way that "labor" also came to refer to the birth process. In English versions of the Holy Bible, "travail" is used to translate a number of original Hebrew and Greek words, some of which refer to birth, while others refer to either heavy labor or a severe experience of any sort.

Stressors are all factors of travails a noun meaning painfully difficult or burdensome work; toil; pain or suffering resulting from mental or physical hardship etc. The effects of travail resemble the agony felt through child birth. Numbers 20:14 of American King James states; "and God sent messenger from Kadesh to the King of Edom, thus saith brother Israel, thou knowest all the travail that hath befallen". So, as it is God knew of all the heavy laden that had fallen upon our family. No more ability to stop every ice cream truck which passed by, governmental food stamps had become our means of food accessibility. No more seasonal cloth shopping sprees, we had to see what was available through care packages and give away. No more family outings to the beaches and parks; well not like they use to be. God bless my mother, she's amongst those of us fortunate enough not to break totally apart due to travail.

Briefly I would like to bring out some realistic factors which contribute to travail hardships and heavy labor, then we can go in and discover how I Trevale met, encountered and deals with travail. Travail is derived of a sinful nature. The act of disobeying and eating the fruit in which God forbid, deemed Eve the affliction of knowing child baring through giving birth in which pain and agony was derived. This is the long suffering of the nine months in which constitutes the baring and delivering of new life, "birth". Isaiah 54:1 of the New American Standard Bible reads; "shout for joy, o barren one, you who have bared no child; break forth into a joyful shouting and cry aloud, you who have not travailed; for the son of the desolate one will be more numerous than the sons of the married women," says the lord. Hmmmmm? So you tell me travail is as a punishment for a woman with no husband? Yes. It is stated of our heavenly creator, the creator of all which exist, John 1:1-3 states of the King James "In the beginning was the word, and the word was with God, and the word was God. The same was in the beginning with God. All things were made by Him and without Him was not anything made that was made. In 1 Corinthians 7:9 of the NIV it is stated; "

however if they cannot control themselves they should get married, for it is better to marry than to burn with passion, where as Genesis 2:24 implies, "for this reason a man shall leave his father and mother and shall cling unto his wife and they shall be one flesh". When this occurs even the front is blessed. Without this structure of unity there come to multitude of short coming, curses and punishments, travail; just as a rode upon thy back. This is just one aspect of what causes travail within the association of relationships. However there are many more and it is safe to say sin and disobedience which causes travail is unnumbered. Yet it is also safe to say that travail is generated as a result of wrongful doings. One may not have sexed out of wed lock, nor murdered nor stole. One may not even be the spectacle of a liar but has still undergone the burdens of travail. Let's face life; if the fly on the wall could speak we may all be in knee deep. It is for told in scripture Romans 3:23 "all has sinned and fall short of the glory of God", just as Eve did in the Garden of Eden, and I did back during my teens and early adulthood.

No one can make Spiritual travail happen; it is introduced at the will of the Holy Spirit because, the Spirit itself makes intercession for us with groaning which cannot be uttered. The Spirit of God is interceding, not us! It is the

Spirit of God bringing life to God's will, which have already been ordained by God. For years, I have experienced travail associated with groaning from the tightening of the muscles, coming upon me at odd times and places, such as before and during church meetings, on the streets, and during conversations with people. I've travailed for other people, and seen them delivered from major spirits. I have undoubtedly travailed for myself. I rarely know what I'm travailing about. This scenario kind of fits; since we know not what we should pray for, as we ought.

Some years ago I had the spirit of fear. It controlled me and would rise up whenever it wanted to. I never discussed the fact that I had it till I searched for psychiatric help near 2003. Fear of failure was what was revealed later, as I was going through my deliverance. This was understandable since I felt that I had failed in everything I had tried to accomplish in this life, even my own suicidal attempts.

$\mathcal{V}$

Lost

Yes, I was lost and for the most of it without a clue, now we are back to the diversity of the community and society in which I was raised. It was time to release all that stuff I was taught to cover up or push to the back burning. It was time for me to deliver what I had learned of anger, aggression, violence and hatred. Yes hatred I had learned as a teen to hate all the things about life that had come upon me; sad to say many can relate.

I was that queen to be, and I wanted my place upon my thrown. The ability to smile; be happy and embraces love peace joy and happiness. Instead I had to learn to keep the house oversee my siblings and attain to my own youthful development. This was while my mother worked to pay the bills and search development coping mechanisms. Methods for depression stress and set back.

Still a daddy's girl and my mom's heaviest burden, I tried to do things myself, attempting to seek out a dad who wasn't even stable. I gave my mother, sister and brother the family blues as a teenage runaway who met many faiths. As a teen on the go I was at times homeless, foodless, and have suffered rape attacks. I still find it hard to except the position of being associated with rape, there are always feelings that it was all my fought and outside of putting it in this book I've tried to keep it to myself. As a teenage runaway, how could I not think it would not have happened if I were not out of place. "I suffered and I cried, I was a disobedient child."

At the age of fifth-teen, after seasons of prayer my mother decided to totally give me over to God since I thought I was grown and knew it all anyway. I was considered by friends and family as a "miss know it all" you would always here them exclaim as I approach here come trouble Tucker, Miss know it all. And yes I was coming and with all the answers and resolutions that I put together with my own fickle mind. "Always talking loud, not knowing anything." As my dad would say, don't even know how to brush my teeth on a regular basis. But in my mind who was he to talk. He couldn't even figure out how to keep his family together even when they were apart, always pushing the blame.

And yes I did that too, push the blame; it was never about what I did but always about other's actions which caused my reactions. Oh I had it good, "I would not have, if you would have not".

Shame on me, but yes Trevale has experience travail as a repercussion of my sins/disobedience too, after three relationships outside of God. In one relationship I was 19-years-old and he was 33-years-old. When we met, I was 3 months pregnant from a previous relationship. This older guy befriended me, cultivated me then moved me in baring a child inside. I respected him for taking me in pregnant and all, housing and providing for me. Little did I know, what was good; two years later would turn bad. So bad that I would have to plan a way to escape and I did. But like what is common in our society I returned over and over again. Till I crossed a man that would marry me and break the cycle of back and forth abuse, mentally and physically. This man was the first guy I married, see it wasn't so much about love, but it was more about breaking a cycle. I was so desperate to break the cycle that I didn't even care that this new guy was incarcerated in the county jail, pending transfer to state prison. Yes you read me right a Queen from the top of the Hill not only got pregnant out of wed lock and fornicated with an older man but married a county/state prisoner without even first holding his hand. See he had game and a bright smile and I made that all worth the while. I traveled our first year of marriage, to and from the prison house. I spent years with him in and out of prisons; for charges ranging from possession, sales and even suspicion of bank robbery. Yes all of that and in each incident he proclaimed it wasn't him, and I stuck with him through it all.

The fifth year brought about an end, but not before he impregnated me with my second child, my son. Like a bandage on an open wound the older guy was there to mend my broken heart. Though at first we didn't make it, this time we were going for the gold. After 4 years of putting things in place and much restoral we married, the older guy and I. We had been together off and on for nine years prior and together brought fourth three more beautiful, healthy, adorable children, another girl and two more boys. I had always been a mother first maybe not the best, but the best I could be with the hand life dealt me, or the life I created for myself.

God always been my refuge and his company has always kept me; even in the mist of my sin which caused travail (long suffering). I couldn't count the number of bruises, busted lips and black eyes I've encounter through many relationships, nor the number of how many I've given. I was taught when someone hit you to hit them back. After witnessing my mom and dad's episodes and many others just like theirs, I kind of imagined it was just life. And no matter what went wrong, soon enough it would be alright, "wrong answer!" Very wrong. Soon enough and not long ago that marriage ended to.

Lost? Yes, that I was for sure, lost in pain from stress, lost in depression, lost in being heavy laden and lost in toil. Travail had encamped itself around and about my every endeavor from family, relationships and child raising, to finances and self consciousness.

Yes, family relationships were jeopardized too, but thanks be it to God, my family understands me better than I do.

As I spent most of my days running behind my boy friends', mates and husbands. I only imagined that each move I made was getting me closer to a stabled relationship. I imagined it was a good move if it directed me to cringe to my man. I thought then and still believe now however, that a woman should walk along side her man. But then I was forsaking the embrace of the loving family I was leaving behind. After each fallen relationship my family was there to assist in placing me back on solid grounds; my mother, my dad, my sister, my brother my grandparents' aunts and uncles. They all have my back even as a disobedient, possibly ungrateful child, all the way to and through adulthood, a family in which you could find true un-judgmental love. Even my cousins had my back. But undoubtedly I wanted the love of a man to call all my own. But not any man. I kept myself waiting first for a strong man, with the ability to maintain the development of a family, wife and kids. Early on in my early adulthood as I join into relations, I didn't mandate the principle of "the love of God FIRST". So once I begin my laboring into the Lord. I begin to identify where my relationship yokes was un-equal. For one I had to not look, but allow myself to be found.

Allowing myself to be found allowed me direction in utilizing the abilities developed to determine how well my inner labors will have paid off, how well my intuitive receptivity will guide me through the unpredictability and distractions of daily life, how well my inner talent translated into decision and action. It's very difficult to remain centered and not get caught up in conflicts and competition. In a situation like this, placing your-self in a quiet place and considering the big picture and not getting taken in by petty disagreements, set backs or taking things personally.

Yes it is a bit difficult to remain centered in these type positions. Hoping there was favor enough from God to bless me with a soul mate. Now was the time for getting my house (self) in order, objectively learning to practice leadership by sponsoring progress and innovation rather than by fighting for control. I had moved myself into a position which suggested that this was a time of establishing stability and security, a much needed break from stressful strivings. However, my situation turned to being somewhat resistant to transformation and progress. My recent surge of creativity had whined down. Again my faithfulness was altered. Outside of allowing myself to hold still for the victory which comes through patients I return to my old flame, the father of my youngest three children; the older guy.

Since we were already divided from being unequally yoked the desires of self empowerment left. I had accepted that the visions I felt were embedded from God Himself were just perceptions of my own and not God's will. So again I set out just accepting whatever came my way. This is including excepting when my x husband, the daddy and assistant provider of all five of our children, whom I loved dearly, impregnated another woman, who brought forth the child while we were still married. Not knowing which way to turn, since I had given God the back seat, Bless Him for not leaving me; I knew that the next project which was yet to be discovered had to be found within.

VI

Finding Self

Surprisingly I have been a worshiper since I was a young child. I was baptized at 9 years old and allowed the presence of the Holy Spirit to fill me at that same time. I surrendered to recognizing the presence of God the father in my life, and being to study the Word (Holy Bible). One thing I learned in regards to our fathers' ways is; we are forever learning. Realizing that there are principles to life and they must be applied to reap the benefits of life.

So now came the time for starting new development in setting solid principles. See early on I had my own set of principle but they were applied with the mindset of a cornel individual. Now it was time for me to apply all my life experiences with the God given principles of life. Yes, time to apply the rod for my own sake. First I listened and read through the words of The Books of Psalms and Proverbs which identified with me my current situations, gave instructions on communicating with God, and how to apply life's experiences to the teachings of God's principles and the direction which followed. In Proverbs, I was informed of the travails which were applied when directions were lost or instructions weren't followed. See, as an adult, I begin to identify travails as a good lashing from God. Like when we don't obey the rules that our parents give us....

For most of us those type actions requires a punishment or rode of some sort.

My Favorite verses in Psalms, is Psalms 23. "The Lord is my Shepherd; I shall not want. He maketh me to lie down in green pastures: he restoreth my soul: he leadeth me in the paths of righteousness for his name's sake. Yea, though I walk through the valley of the shadow of death, I will fear no evil: for thou art with me; thy rod and thy staff they comfort me. Thou prepare a table before me in the presence of mine enemies: thou anoints my head with oil; my cup runneth over. Surely goodness and mercy shall follow me all the days of my life: and I will dwell in the house of the Lord forever". There is so much life and reassurance in just those 6 verses.... As God the shepherd watches over me I learn that I would want for nothing. I rest in the comfort of a home, with green pastures. I receive newness each day. The word is my guide. Even in my darkest hours, he is with me. My enemies see me blessed, as if I have more than enough and God's grace and mercy is ever lasting. As I mediated that daily, I begin to be filled with the security of God's presence. Proverbs helps me to identify the works of the wise and of fools and their actions there in.

Then I surfaced "Job," wondering how one man could stand so strong on his beliefs when those close to him urged him to turn away for a new revelation. It appeared to me, Job knew like the story foretold, the enemy could not touch Job or his worth without the ok from God. Job knew that no matter what crime or incident, it was all of God good on bad for the edifying of His Will. Through Job patients and faith God was able to restore all that the enemy had taken and destroyed. Given Job a life better than the one before. The greatest notion I received from the book of Job in finding myself was; to not fear, not even of my passed for what the enemy set for bad God will deliver good.

So ok, now I knew based on Malachi 3:11-12 that God would rebuke the devourers for me, that the fruit of my grounds would not be destroyed. God promised that nations would call me blessed and I shall delight in the land forever. This is where I begin to build my hope. See God had kept me through the tribulations which I endured baring travail to the up most. ~His grace and mercy kept me.~ Even though I had become aware that the spiritual battle was won, (Jesus on the Cross), as a back slider I still choose to fight battles on my own. Year in and year out I couldn't grasp the notion of Kingdom Living. So I fought the fight the best I knew how not letting anyone take no advantage or walkover me.

The enemy knew my weakness feeling incomplete without a man. So through my relationships he stayed close to me. The enemy taunted me to renounce my trust, faith and belief in God. Sub doing all consciousness to the trust that my mate would provide my every need, as long as I followed his lead. The enemy taunted me to embrace a mate who struggled to put trust in God first, even more so "Jesus on the Cross". Since I couldn't make since of it, I became more unstable, knowing not weather I was coming and going. So I retracted back to what I embraced as a teenager, to sub do the feelings of emptiness. I fell into a life of drinking and smoking herbs. Sad to say, I didn't like neither as a joy, but the enemy (negative thinking) which influenced me to think it was a resource for empting my enthusiasm in life and overcoming my depression pain and anxiety.

Soon enough I too spent time in county jails for domestic violence and child abuse allegations (found not guilty). Though my longest stay was only 6 days without a conviction, to me it was hard time leaving my young children to wonder my faith. And the shame, oh let's not mention the shame of whose known to be a true believer, community activist and family support life skill counselor; arrested for abuse on others.

Though I was on a search to find myself I found myself losing it over and over again. So what I learned so far is no matter what, the enemy (negative influences) will not quit, and is not distant until the second coming of our Lord and Savior. There are lots of fact findings in finding ones' self. One is that you can't avoid becoming; and will only become who you are created by God and self to be.

VII

Ignoring the Call of Life

This brings about some literature or spoken word which God placed in my spirit along the way. It has, in part been spoken at inspirational engagements, within the house which ministers the gospel of life, family reunions and evangelism witnessing. It has been often spoken in gatherings and witnessing to homeless and needy. It is titled and reads:

LIFE, IGNORING THE CALL

I suffered and I cried; I was a disobedient child. I went through trials and tribulations; he said sit and pray for a while. Life had no meaning every issue was a trail and do to my disobedience I fell for a while. I was told to sit still, I desired to stand. Through his grace and his mercy he still took my hand. I was told to be patient not to rush or I'd crash. Being who I was I knew I could handle my task. Yet again I fall face down to the floor, I could hear him say DAUGHTER JUST HOW MUCH MORE? I'M BIGGER THAN THAT I SAID THAT'S JUST NOT MY FIELD AND AGAIN WITHOUT GOD, I TOOK ANOTHER SPILL. Frustration set in but I was determined to win so again without god, I took another spine. I'm doing well now that was just not my way, and again came darkness which filled the whole place. SIT

STILL MY CHILD He said THIS IS NOT YOUR WAY!
Then everything went black. There's not much more to
say. I'm bigger then this, Educated the Best amongst the
rest. Yet there I was again calling for someone else to get
me out of my own mess. Wisdom cried out. I heard her
from afar, knowledge sat waiting right beside my liquor
bar. My body's now wounded, weary broken in two, my
bar is not pleasant, I'm lost knowing not what to do. A
dark shadow appeared and starred me face to face and in
that moment time I realized I must clean up this place. So
I fell to the floor but with no disgrace, for I knew once
more the floor must meet my face. I cried in repentance I
cried unto the Lord, have Mercy on me Father for I
cannot take no more .He said my child come walk with me
for in your repentance I am very pleased. I will give you
contentment in place of greed, patients to suppress the
notions of need. That dark of travail shall be removed and
an assurance spirit placed within for a new creature in
Christ within the spiritual realm is where you shall begin.

Walk by faith not by sight

Gaining those things that be not as though they are

Believing that all things can be done through Christ

which strengthen you

For the lord is your Sheppard and you shall not want

Upon this rock you shall build a house and the gates of hell shall not prevail.
Be blessed those whom have heard and received the message of the lord.
Through my spoken testimony
AMEN

God's way exemplifies health and natural joy in the body, the science of healing arts, music and all things good, true and beautiful. We develop our fondest and greatest ideals from God. As directed of God, I journey to share my views so others can unite with me, volunteer to help and offer to provide framework for a united team. God has chosen my inspiration, enthusiasm and leadership to bear fruit. It is imperative that I design a plan of action. I am in a position to be generous with my time. Generosity is always a win/win.

There is a warm feeling in the power of giving; it improves your reputation while others are being helped and so on. In ignoring the call to generate generosity unto Gods house and his works, I could imagine many have felt and reacted in this same way: watching out for those endeavors that cause you to be hooked to obligation or the seeds of ongoing dependency, in turn creating a moral dilemma only the very high-minded can manage well. I don't know about others, but though my motives tend to be good, finding balance between kindness and accountability has always been a struggle for me.

My struggles have been finding that balance, so in "Ignoring the Call"; I chose to stay out of the forefront to avoid the conflicts of moral dilemmas'. How well did that work? I guess you're wondering. Well it didn't work at all. I stayed stagnate in that one place where God met me and delivered the message to Evangelize. I remained left there till I turned, grabbed my cross and took direction. For me this brought Life, Purpose and all. Nobody said the road would be easy or that the sun would always shine. But it's said no matter what you go through, he'll be with you all the time. That! I had to trust and believe in. I was ready for something different in life, so I had to make different choices. Moral and ethical dilemmas' had to get behind. I was done with the suffering and crying. "Yes Father, I am Here"

VIII

Evangelism

Evangelism is the preaching of the Christian Gospel or the practice of relaying information about a particular set of beliefs to others with the object of conversion. Christians who specialize in evangelism are known as evangelists whether they are in their home communities or living as missionaries in the field. Some Christian traditions consider evangelists to be in a leadership position; they may be found preaching to large meetings or in governance roles. Christian groups who actively encourage evangelism are sometimes known as evangelistic or evangelist. The scriptures do not use the word evangelism, but evangelist is used in the translations of Ephesians 4:11 And he gave some, apostles; and some, prophets; and some, evangelists; and some, pastors and teachers;.... and 2 Timothy 4:5 But watch thou in all things, endure afflictions, do the work of an evangelist, make full proof of thy ministry.

Evangelism has been a part of my life and a token of what I have exercised for as far back as I can remember. As a child I often evangelized to my peers the Word of God and His Commandments, in the beginning God made everything. Even though my days of evangelism begin when I was young, I didn't receive acknowledgement till my early 30's. Known for spreading messages relevant to the gospel and salvation of Christ on the Cross, directing and encouraging souls into salvation through God's Love Peace Joy Restoration and Happiness; God has always provided me with the means of life. I cannot complain. When I obeyed, God rewarded me, when I disobeyed, punishment was allowed to come upon me through travail.

God's unchanging love never failed me. Even during seasons in which sin directed me away from mission and my purpose. It was my choice position to operate half delivered and half not. Meaning I was willing to let go of something's, but others I kept, and I kept it to myself. Like living half Holy and half sinner; having one foot in and one foot out of the realm of Holy faithfulness. See I churched during service hours and joining excessive un-Godly gatherings and parties, eating and leisure times and attempted to combine the activities. I soon realized that the example I was setting was that of a hypocrite and before judgment could enter the atmosphere, I begin judging myself, pulling myself out of ministries in which God had assigned me for his purpose.

This caused me to become my worst enemy. Dropping into solitary and blaming myself for everything. The enemy needed not come forth regarding me anymore; he assured I did a good job at attacking myself. So for seven years I did just that. Till from worry and travail, as I begin sinking myself into deep depression, I begin reaching to God from the pits of hell. Well that's what life felt like as I endured travail (long suffering); I was lead to apply James 1:2 concept of patients, "My brethren, count it all joy when ye fall into divers temptations; knowing this, that the trying of your faith worketh patience. But let patience have her perfect work, that ye may be perfect and entire, wanting nothing."

In addition through my travail (heavy laden) I studied more seeking the Word of God for direction and instructions. Falling into Ecclesiastes 4:6 which reads, "better is a handful with quietness, than both the hands full with travail and vexation of spirit." I begin to stay in the shadows and keep quiet. At the kid's games, I was quiet. At the family gatherings, I became quiet. At work, school and even church, I became quiet. I quieted myself so that I didn't feel I was operating in existence. For many years, even through my evangelism, I felt like the walking dead. Though I kept my shortcomings and unrighteousness to myself, travail still knew where to find me. I would be at the crossroads trying to find my way home.

"Be still My Child and I will Show You the Way". Yes that's what I heard my father say, but being still left me feeling shocked and flattened, which however, was understandable and acceptable. During that time of surrendering and allowing my body mind and soul to be used of the Holy Spirit it was to my best interest not to try to do anything about my conditions nor circumstances at that time, all my worries and concerns had to be passed onto God, and I had to surrender my flesh to lifeless. I surrendered into the inevitable where as whatever happened, happened. I had to undoubtedly put divine trust in God.

I was then again tempted by way of enduring a diverse manner of raising 3-5 children within unstapled relationships. My trust was in the assurance that in time I would recover, and again have some wind behind my sail. But dealing with reality just knocked me out. I had to admit it and go with it -- what else could I have done, my faith was in God. Along with His Word, He directed me through saying "Go", as was stated in 2 Timothy 4:1, 2 &5, to Timothy by Paul; "I charge thee therefore before God, and the Lord Jesus Christ, who shall judge the quick and the dead at his appearing in his kingdom; Preach the word; be instant in season and out of season; reprove, rebuke, exhort with all longsuffering and doctrine. But watch thou in all things, endure afflictions do the work of an evangelist, make full proof of thy ministry.... A call in which I had to surrender and begin to exercise there in. Evangelism!

IX

Still Here

A testimony for many and mine too is; yes! "I am still here", from a divers childhood, to a terrifying young adult hood to my unstable mid life crises ventures operating in and out of faith. "I am still here". I've been through fire and flames, no literally I suffered and yet was blessed from a totally house fire early 2010, leaving my 4 out of 5 children and myself homeless. I can truly say that when God stepped in and moved me (flesh, self) out, He did just that! It appeared to me that when I became emotionally paralyzed and was not making good decision that God saw fit to step down from his thrown and operate directly in my life fixing things on my behalf Himself. At this point travail had gotten the best of my body mind and soul. Accepting fire as a sign of sterilizing, cleaning & refining, God saw fit to give me a new beginning, again. I had just balanced my way through the first 30 years of travail, enduring my brain injury; severe head concussion and over 6 months of sever amnesia. These occurrences have been requiring thus far 10 years plus recovery. Then I've tried for 10 more years to get my house (myself) in order." Life Ignoring the Call" still! The three troubled marriages and "a misunderstood teen"! For many unaware; misunderstood is the new rational for disobedient. I too was misunderstood! Any way through all the trials and tribulations I'm still here. But now with a purpose!

X

Purpose

Those who are mystically inclined may view the purpose of travailing as coming from God or a Higher Self; others may see it as the springing forth of agitating endeavors and situations causing suffering, agony and pain. In any case, purpose lies around an unfailing source of comfort, assuring the thrown of God. Support, for in this life we think we've seen it all, time and purpose is to send knowledge to heavy laden trouble individuals. In doing so I unveil the pain and suffering of my days, in this book and books, sitcoms and plays, to come. I will explore more into the travail of modern days for the purpose of caring support. What's so sad in regards to this journey is I see travail every day within the faces of many including believers. As many travail and cry out, living lives full of doubt and low self esteem; I find it hard to sit back and see the same things which happened to me happen to them.

The purpose is for getting individuals to embrace karma since it is written in the stars, what goes around comes around. I had to learn that it didn't matter what people said and done, it was up to me not to let them get me down. Like similar words of one of my favorite artist support songs, "I had to lose my fear so I could obtain my breakthrough". Like many I've went through the same thoughts of giving up, I've looked over many edging but did not jump. The only way I could sum it up is I didn't let travail keep me down. Yes it did get me down but bless God my ways of escape turn them around. Then there is optimism which portrays the world as good and beautiful, instead of out of control and brutal. The most important purpose would be to form unity, providing plenty for all and the environment. This fountain of love pours over everything in life. Purpose is to be as a reminder in encouraging individuals to attend to their ventures carefully. Giving hope by encouraging that we take an investment in time, energy, ideas and willpower; plus give attention to details of following-through, to take travail from its infancy to a full-fledged state of achievement and reward. In doing so, allowing all heavy laden, struggles, labor, pain etc; to bring forth the abundance of wisdom and knowledge unto the people of life.

XI

Self Consciousness

God equips us, believers of the Power of Christ with the ability to bring forth healing to others. Ultimately this is according to ones faith and ability to stay before God and ready to act. I remember my first calling to demonstrate the works which God through his word said I had the ability of doing. I watch a miracle right before my eyes, by my own hands and I must say even as a believer, I was amazed. While I may not be the first one to become a doctor or to conduct a lying on of the hands, I have witnessed and is convinced I bring much rejuvenation to others. The way I do this is simple: it's with my faith, trust, laughter, fun-loving way, and ability to see the lighter side of dark days. In all things I pray seeking understanding along the way. Is it easy? Heavens No! But I have found that believing through prayer is the way to go.

Healing is a process, not an event. It is essential to be patient and persevere. To me timing is everything since our work is nothing without God. I would doubt anyone who's a believer would want to operate without God's company. When God allowed me to be a part of that miraculous healing, it was then my self-consciousness begin to grow. Being confident that God was not only with me but also living large within me, gave me the confidents that's surely I could do all things through Christ Philippians 4:13. For the development of self-consciousness I focus my will and repeat solutions. I always try to keep in my remembrance that too much is as bad as too little, as I keep things in balance, slowly and steadily changing the composition of my energy from the old to the new.

A new journey of discovery has begun taking place and now I am positioning myself to embark upon new opportunities with optimism and high spirits. In this position I have applied readiness for a voyage of discovery. I am prepared for the journey, my effects are in order, I'm in great shape and the excitement of venture prevails through the self-consciousness of my ability to achieve.

Inside me there is a powerful feeling of youthful idealism, as well as a bit of daring endeavors. I have no idea if this is going to be difficult or not, but I know those problems are tomorrow's problems. Today my energy is high, spirits are bright, the sky is clear and if there ever was a noble impulse in me, I am getting a chance to express it now. It really helps when other close to you share in that overcoming illusion. I call it an illusion because I truly feel we are built by the impulse which covers our surrounding.

It is a great notion to steer away from co-dependency, especially when you are attempting to rebuild morals and integrity. But it serves a person well to have a support system to encourage them along the way. Today God has sent me a support system which have undoubtedly taken my best interest at hand and in doing so has encourage me to tackle obstacle which I let steal joy and accomplishment right from me. I can't get to far off into what this support system has done for me body mind and soul, because it is up to me to seek being whole. However I'll re-write it in a poem which a very special person wrote and read to me. This poem is very comforting to my soul and exhibits what he feels I do for him and others today. These words to me help in the process of rebuilding my self-conscious mode.

Spirit

It is said there are Angels in Heaven above,
And they shine with the Light of an Inner Love.
Of these things I had not a clue,
But that was before I found You.
For in You I've found
A love that is so Right,
It shines all around with the Brightest of Light.
It comes from somewhere so deep within.
That it has no beginning,
And knows no end.

Your Love is a Light
That brightens each Day
Of all of the people
You see on your way.
Where ever you go
Or whatever you do,
I see the Love that you have inside of You.
That God sent you here with
To a place where you'd be
Sharing such Love with someone like Me.
This is proof for Me
That Angels exist and are filled with a Love
That no man could resist.
I thank God each day for finding the time
And looking down on Me
And making You Mine.
So yes there are Angels
In Heaven above,
I know because
God sent me You to Love.
My Angel Spirit!
Writer: Ole'Dean (Dean) Outland
Contribution to Self Conscious Awareness

XII

Earth, Fire & Wind

Revive, renewed, refreshed; life's beginning in the earth, travail the fire and the winds which sets free. In setting the stage we have accepted; Genesis 2:7 which explains the creation of man at the beginning of time. This verse reads "the LORD God formed the man from the dust of the ground and breathed into his nostrils the breath of life, and the man became a living being". God gave us the earth in which we were made and all there in.

The tongue is a flame of fire. It is a whole world of wickedness, corrupting your entire body. It can set your whole life on fire, for it is set on fire by hell itself. Isaiah 50:11 But now, all you who light fires and provide yourselves with flaming torches, go, walk in the light of your fires and of the torches you have set ablaze. This is what you shall receive from my hand: You will lie down in torment.

"Never be lacking in zeal, but keep your spiritual fervor, serving the Lord" (Romans 12:11). "Do not put out the Spirit's fire" (1 Thessalonians 5:19). Ezekiel 37:9 Then he said to me, "Prophesy to the breath; prophesy, son of man, and say to it, 'This is what the Sovereign LORD says: Come from the four winds, O breath, and breathe into these slain, that they may live."

Ecclesiastes 11:5 As you do not know the path of the wind, or how the body is formed in a mother's womb, so you cannot understand the work of God, the Maker of all things. "The wind blows where it wishes and you hear the sound of it, but do not know where it comes from and where it is going; so is everyone who is born of the Spirit."

Bringing all thing unto understanding under the Sun/Son. Let these scripture be a light unto your way, that your desire to obtain salvation through overcoming travail want be in vain, always remembering these thing which were dropped in my spirit as I struggled to reverse the physical reality of being burn of the earth, burned with fire and cooled by the wind, by unveiling the reality of peace, love and patience. Life is within.

PEACE

In offering the sacrifice of peace,
an offering made by suffering unto the LORD;
We shall certainly return in peace.
So hearken, take heed all people,
For you shall be in leagues with hero's and champions,
un-movable:
and the beasts of the field shall be at peace with you.
Lay down in peace, and sleep:
for our LORD, only make for us to dwell in safety.
Depart from evil, and do good; seek peace, and pursue it.

We looked for peace, at times no good comes;
and through a time of disturbing health we behold
trouble!
Follow righteousness, faith, charity and peace,
with them all things are called to be a pure heart.

LOVE

There is great peace for they which love thy law:
and nothing shall offend them.
Who shall separate us from the love of Christ? Not
tribulation, nor
distress, nor persecution, nor famine,
nor nakedness, nor peril, no not even the sword.
Through hope be not ashamed; because the love of God is
shed
abroad in our hearts by the Holy Ghost which is given to
us.
Seeing you have purified your souls in obeying the truth
through
the Spirit unto unfeigned love of the brethren,
see that you love one another with a pure heart fervently.
Love your enemies, bless them that curse you,
do good to them that hate you,
and pray for them which despitefully use you, and
persecute you.

PATIENCE

Fulfill the royal law according to the scripture;
you shall love thy neighbor as thyself.
The God of patience and consolation shall grant you to be

likeminded one toward another according to Christ Jesus.
For you shall be on good ground, being honest and with a
good heart, having heard the word.
Keep it, and bring forth fruit with patience.
Bow down in worshipped to the Lord, saying:
Lord, have patience with me, for peace is from within.
Rest in the LORD, *and wait patiently for him: fret not*
thyself
because of him who prospered in his own ways,
for a man who brings wicked devices for gain
passes at his own hand.
There is glory when you are suffered for your own faults,
yet you take it patiently.
For when you do well, and suffer for it (travail), taking it
patiently,
you demonstrate what is acceptable with God.

Inspired of the Holy Scriptures

XIII

Trevale

My Deliverance.

Journeying a little closer into my life, I reflect on my teen age years in visualizing the effects of my parents' divorce. I found it even harder to cope being the oldest, and my sister and brother's keeper. Most often in every family there is one whom considers him/her self as the black sheep of that family. That one person that no one else seems to understand. Between teen age and young adulthood, I considered myself that black sheep. Being held so responsible over many matters at young ages and not gaining the social curriculum training needed for community and communication involvement, I shank deeper and deeper into my own black hole of low self esteem, blaming everyone else for my lack of social socialization.

Prior to my parent divorce we were forced to relocate separating me from my grade school child hood friends. It was like moving to a new country even though it was a mile away. For whatever reason, I had always found it hard to make friends and as a teenager that was something I didn't wish to indulge in all over again. I was born a scorpion according to the zodiac sign. This is a zodiac known to display projection a mean demeanor individual. I imagine do to life experiences I projected a demeanor of

87

being mean. This is possibly why my grandfather called me "Little Trouble Tucker". My old friend from early youth had managed to bypass my forward attitude and they often accepted me as I was, bitter and controlling. Since we were basically tots' starting out they learn to just let me be me. Though I was primary the tallest and for most of it at times the larges, in reality unless I was taunted I wouldn't have hurt a fly. But my mean angry look intimidated many so they just stayed away. Of those whom did attempt befriending me I was very choosing of whom I wanted in my circle so that number stayed low. I found it better to have one to three good friends then a gang of mouths talking load and saying nothing. So there I was as a teenager always with one good friend on my side. I didn't know if it was for the good of making it easier to ship through trouble undetected or alleviating witness who creators weren't at my best interest.

As a teen I begin to slip through the cracks of obedience. Many would want to say it was because I had a disruptive upbringing. I'd like to be downright honest, I was curious and disobedient. Yes I had unbarring pressures but the bottom line was I lacked nothing. That is something that one does not realize until they have lost everything. At the age thirteen I began to smoke marijuana. I knew it was not for children, teenagers neither but a cousin started me selling single joints and after smoking one or two, I was hooked. I guess you can say I began to get high on my own supplies. It wasn't soon after that when my straight "A" report cards went straight to D's and F's. Then at age 15 my Cool Aid smile turned into Old English breathe; beer that is. I now know that marijuana forms a since of paranoia. I always felt someone was watching me. I was so vain; everything had to be about me good or bad. Many say these actions stemmed from my abusive pass as a child, so I rolled with it, even though I knew better. I was either high or drunk, as a teenager.

Being rebellion and refusing to follow my mother's commands I became a teenager runaway. This too started around age 13. When I should have been learning proper self assurance and that pertain to good mental growth, I was rolling blunts and drinking beer and trying to be what I thought society wanted to see. So I sported my freak mama jeans, members only jacket with "Ms. Pimpin Ass Peaches" printed on the back and became my own role model. I was never a school dropout; the fact is some teachers dropped me from class for non attendance though. Thankfully there was my clueless mother getting me back in class over and over again. See I love my mother dearly but it benefited me in a bitter sweet way that she's one of those mothers whose children do no wrong. So it was always everyone else fault when I got sent home when the majority of the time I was dead wrong. My mother saved me from many F's through her associated teaching profession, which would have for sure set me back.

I call my mother clueless in a passive way, since what mother truly wants to imagine there precious daughters going astray. But I was straying and straying further away. Though I had boyfriends at young ages I didn't really start to date till the age of 15. Now that I am an adult I realize that it was too early even then. As fast as I was at 15 I was dating a 25 year old man. I told him I was 18 and I told my parents he was 19. That lie created lies and lies after lies. As grown as I thought I was nothing can express the feelings I had when he mandated that we finally engage sexually. After bickering and crying, coming up with every excuse imaginable, I did everything but tell this 25 year old man the truth. I was only 15 years old. So nothing I said moved him to stop his aggressiveness towards me and with one incident I was pregnant. I kept it a secret but not for long cause my 25 year old boyfriend was planning to take me home, to Texas that is. It was time for the truth because after I was forced to indulge in the act of sex I was afraid of the man. So I prolong and delayed this venture till finally I told him my age. After I told him my true age he had mixed emotions, as he explained, in his mind he was in love and expecting his first child. What a mess my lies had made. The older guy insisted I tell my mother because by then he really wanted me to go to Texas. Tell my mother; What? Now that was going to be hard, but to my surprise, hard made easy. She knew right away I wasn't ready and that my baby had to be returned to God.

How here I was, all of a sudden wanted to bring religion into the scenario after all I had been doing. I was telling my mother, "Abortion is against our religion". As if smoking weed and drinking wasn't! Not to mention the lying, fighting and the cursing. I stressed my mother having her chase after me for like two months to keep appointment with the doctors. I finally surrender and prayed, then let my mother have her way or God for that matter. Though I hated what had to be done I knew I wasn't ready for a child anyway.

Sad to say at that time, that didn't slow me down, but it sped me up. Since I came to know sex and pregnancy through that one incident, I thought I was more grown than ever. Because my mother was still guardian over me and the rules were stricter as the chores grew many, I decided to become a true runaway. Leaving home, then chasing after my dad, sleeping in abandon buildings and broken down cars, eating whatever, whenever. I stayed in school though, and when there was not school I hung out around the way. Many times I snuck in and out of my own home when my mother and grandparent were asleep. I got clean cloths and a bit to eat. Till one day my grandfather (RIP) caught me trying to sneak in from the pool house through the back door, into the kitchen. "Trail (my nickname then) he called, aren't you tired? I've seen you creep in and out for some time now and your mother is worried sick. The best thing is for you to come on home and repent". And so I did.

Life became more and more challenging being raised with a single parent and not much extra money. When my mother met more difficult times it seemed like all the pressures were on me. I did repent and I did change my ways. There was no drinking or any smoking for the rest of my teenage days, but depression was still the same. Cutting down on my freedom, due to disobedience, made my responsibilities at home increase. Trying to do right and bring my grades up and being a decent child with a decent life was the most challenging. Turning 16 was senseless to me. I had dreams but couldn't see them coming through so suicide was the best thing I could do.

In the middle of the afternoon after being chastised for not cleaning after others in the home I went into the medicine cabinet and took every prescribed medicine my grandparents owned. I said a prayer and went to sleep, for all I knew that was the end of me. No more whippings chastising too. No more bad decisions trying to see how I'd make it through, at last the world would have been done with me, the little black sheep with low self-esteem, and soon I would be done with the world too. The weirdest thing occurred I slept for two days not even getting up to use the restroom. My mother didn't even wake me up for school. I guess she thought I needed the rest, till the second day when my five year old brother's school called her from her job. She had to get my brother because I was still stuck in bed. It was like a coma; I could hear but could not respond. I wondered why I was still here, not awake but totally numb.

My mother crashed the house (came in with range) "your lazy ass can't just lay here all day get your ass up and clean this house now today". Numbed or not I had to move so with everything in me I rolled myself out of the bed. Thirsty I went to the fridge for some water as I opened it everything went black my eyes were blinded as a dark hole appeared before me, and a voice spoke to me and told me to "reach in". The voice was saying "isn't this the way you want to go"? I cried into the Lord in repentance as I called out to family saying "help I can't see, help I took pills". "The devil is taking me". My grandmother, a well known church mother and pastor began to anoint my eyes and pray aloud. A time after her continuous praying, as the paramedics were on their way, my sight began to return, life returned, I lived to see another day. After that things got sweet. I had a second chance to continue life.

Situation was kind of the same but now I had another plan. I became a dreamer since life to me was a mess; I spent most of my time dreaming of a life worth living. I did this throughout the remaining years of my teens and all the way till I was able to be on my own. Then came relationships and the dreaming had to vanish. I had troubled relationships not one or two or three or four times or better. Today I'm set aside with 5 children and three baby daddies. My longest relationship was twenty two years. Seven of the years I was married, this was with the older guy mentioned earlier in the book, the father of 3 of my wonder children. For something to last that long one might say it was love. And that it was. Undying love, not so, since it died after twenty two years or more. Money, it is known to be the root to all evil; the love of money that is. It appeared then that I had a nick for older guys'. I now see it was the father I lost that I wanted to see in them. I say that with no disrespect. For I do appreciate the roles of the older guys in my life, especially for the children I carried and brought forth.

This brings us again to self conscious awareness. I had to stop looking for someone to make me feel complete. I had to embrace my life as if it was a treat, no matter what. I had to dominate every obstacle that I met. And I had to change my way of thinking for it had gotten me no where yet. Now it was time for me to be me. To take off the mask and see all I could see.

There is now no need for the saturation of one opinion on me. Fear has gone, I have been set free. The "what if's" aren't controlling me anymore. My body still ached from the reality of being torn but that to will heal. Rest, eating right and filling my spirit with Godly Praise and Worship in the Word of God are my substantial tools. Looking back at my experiences, I understand more of what Paul meant when he said,"...I travail in birth again until Christ be formed in you." Jesus had no fear in Him, so if Christ had been formed in me, fear had to go!

I give glory to God who sent the Holy Spirit, Whose works are beyond our imaginations. I've been on both ends of travail and I've learned through my years that if I yield to the travail that comes my way, it will always bring forth a change, a good result, and fruit. Travail brings life! It's the Holy Spirit doing it, not ours.

Before closing I would like to invite you to join the family of believer as we reverence Christ for Salvation. It is simply based on your Admitting to the sins which causes travail, Believing in Christ and his Death on the Cross, that our sins are forgiven and Confessing your Faith in God. Once this is established within your heart, behold you are a new creature in Christ, Old things are passed away and all things has become new. Amen!

May the Peace of God be with You.

Love Peace Joy and Happiness

ABOUT THE AUTHOR

T.L. "Spirit" Tucker

In giving a detailed description and account of my life story, I have delivered more than basic facts regarding my education, works, relationships and gain and lose experiences. My life's sub-sequential endeavors portray subject experiences of each event. Unlike my profile, my story presents a subject life story, highlighting various aspects of my encounters; including intimate details of experiences and the analyzing of my personality.

As a Business Management and Human Service Major, taking part in my Counseling ability, I have designed methods of delivering assistance through passionate story, sitcom and litetour writings. Much of my written told stories and literature works are usually non-fiction, but fiction can also be used to portray extra aspects and spectacle views of life. I give special thanks to CLF Publishing, LLC. (Dr. Cassundra White-Elliott) for assisting in obtaining the written permission, cooperation and participation associated with publishing and presenting my book.